Summary of

The Common Good
Robert B. Reich

Conversation Starters

By BookHabits

Please Note: This is an unofficial Conversation Starters guide. If you have not yet read the original work, you can purchase the original book here.

Copyright © 2018 by BookHabits. All Rights Reserved. First Published in the United States of America 2018

We hope you enjoy this complementary guide from BookHabits. Our mission is to aid readers and reading groups with quality, thought provoking material to in the discovery and discussions on some of today's favorite books.

Disclaimer / Terms of Use: This guide is unofficial and unauthorized. It is not authorized, approved, licensed, or endorsed by the original book's author or publisher and any of their licensees or affiliates. Product names, logos, brands, and other trademarks featured or referred to within this publication are the property of their respective trademark holders and are not affiliated with BookHabits. The publisher and author make no representations or warranties with respect to the accuracy or completeness of these contents and disclaim all warranties such as warranties of fitness for a particular purpose.
No part of this publication may be reproduced or retransmitted, electronic or mechanical, without the written permission of the publisher.

Bonus Downloads
*Get Free Books with **Any Purchase** of* Conversation Starters!

Every purchase comes with a FREE download!

Add spice to any conversation
Never run out of things to say
Spend time with those you love

Get it Now

or Click Here.

Scan Your Phone

Tips for Using Conversation Starters:

EVERY GOOD BOOK CONTAINS A WORLD FAR DEEPER THAN the surface of its pages. Questions herein are designed to bring us beneath the surface of the page and invite us into the world that lives on. These questions can be used to:

- Foster a deeper understanding of the book
- Promote an atmosphere of discussion for groups
- Assist in the study of the book, either individually or corporately
- Explore unseen realms of the book as never seen before

Table of Contents

Introducing *The Common Good* 6

Discussion Questions 14

Introducing the Author 35

Fireside Questions 41

Quiz Questions 52

Quiz Answers 65

Ways to Continue Your Reading 66

Introducing *The Common Good*

The Common Good written by Robert B. Reich takes a close look at America's eroded state of civic life, how it has deteriorated through the years as a result of the loss of connectedness among citizens, and explores this common connection which used to hold the country together. It discusses the common good, particularly the shared ideals and principles that Americans had, and how this can be restored.

Reich starts the book by citing the example of Martin Shkreli, an immigrant from Albania who earned a business degree and got wealthy through fraudulent means. All throughout his trial, he mocked the jurors and journalists, and bragged on social media that he will be declared not guilty. He was convicted on eight counts. Reich says Shkreli exemplifies what has gone wrong in American society today, with people doing things that go against the common good becoming the norm. He defines common good by citing the shared values and ideals that make society a fair and just place for its citizens. He disputes Ayn Rand's philosophy of selfishness that is upheld by many of today's leaders and says that to the contrary the country has witnessed common good in action in the years after World War II. Back then, government and citizens funded public good in terms of schools, roads, and healthcare; and the rights of African Americans and women were recognized. To stress how people have increasingly violated the common good over the years, he gives a timeline of events starting in the 1960s to the present, where particular individuals and groups created widespread distrust in society through their selfish actions. Reich believes that the common good can be still be restored despite the breakdown in shared values and ideals. It has to start with leaders in government, business, and civil society who accept their responsibility of rebuilding public trust in the institutions they serve. He also suggests using the age-old tradition of honoring people and behaviors which promote the common good and shaming behaviors that erode it.

But these have to be done wisely because history shows tyrants and demagogues have destroyed reputations of people who were brave enough to expose the truths about them. This is especially true in this age of social media. Another way to support common good is to take responsibility for insisting on public truth. This not only involves the regular citizen but those in positions as fact-checkers, reporters, and whistle-blowers who could also be serving as scientists, analysts, and professors. He especially cites public lying done by American presidents as behavior that has contributed much to public distrust. Another way to restoring common good is teaching children their civic duty as citizens who will uphold shared values and ideals.

They need to learn respect for institutions, know how to deliberate what best serves society, and how to disagree without disrespecting others' opposing opinions.

The book briefly and effectively tackles the theme of common good in a clear and approachable way, with 209 pages that explain the topic in three parts and ten chapters. Part One, "What is the Common Good," explores and defines the topic, including its history. He quotes political thinkers like Edmunde Burke, Vaclav Havel, and novelist George Orwell who uphold the ideals of a just society, in opposition to the ideas of Ayn Rand whose ideas of selfishness are also well-explained. Part Two, "What Happened to the Common Good?"

includes three chapters on how selfishness among business and government leaders have increasingly become the norm from the 60's to the present. Reich provides a long list of incidents that detail how public trust was repeatedly violated. This includes The Pentagon Papers in 1971, the Savings and Loans Scandals in the 1980s and 90s, The Iran-contra Scandal in 1986, the Government Shutdown in 1995, and more recently the Wells Fargo Scandal in 2017. Part Three entitled "Can the Common Good Be Restored?" takes four chapters to explore ways on how citizens can bring back public trust in democratic institutions and restore the common good. Reich provides interesting stories which serve to highlight his points. In discussing what good leadership is all about he tells the case of Senator John McCain, who flew to Washington from Arizona despite ongoing treatment for brain cancer, to vote against the repeal the Affordable Care Act of July 2017. He quotes him delivering his admonishments to Congress to put the people's welfare above selfish interests. The sub-theme of American identity in relation to common good is explained, with Reich stressing that it is not color or language that makes the American identity but the commitment to the shared values that promote equal access to justice and economic opportunity. A list of recommended reading is provided at the end of the book, along with a discussion guide. These serve to help readers further explore the issues raised in the book.

The Common Good is the latest book written by Reich whose bestselling books include *Supercapitalism, Locked in the Cabinet,* and *Saving Capitalism.*

Discussion Questions

"Get Ready to Enter a New World"

Tip: Begin with questions dealing with broader issues to ensure ample time for quality discussions. Read through all discussion questions before engaging.

~~~

question 1

Martin Shkreli, an immigrant from Albania, is cited by Reich as an example of the erosion of common good. What acts did Shkreli do that exemplifies violation of the common good?

~~~

question 2

Reich says people doing things that go against the common good has become the norm. How does he define the common good?

~~~

question 3

He disputes Ayn Rand's philosophy of selfishness that is upheld by many of today's leaders. Who among today's leaders believe in Rand's philosophy?

~~~

question 4

Rand believes that there is no such thing as common good. What is Reich's argument against this? What example does he cite?

~~~

question 5

Reich says people have increasingly violated the common good over the years. How does he support this claim?

~~~

~~~

question 6

According to Reich, the common good can be still be restored despite the breakdown in shared values and ideals. Do you agree with him? Why? Why not?

~~~

~~~

question 7

He says restoring common good starts with leaders in government, business, and civil society. What can leaders do to rebuild public trust in the institutions they serve?

~~~

question 8

He cites public lying done by American presidents as behavior that has contributed much to public distrust. Can you cite examples of presidents who lied? How did you know they were lying?

~~~

~~~

question 9

Reich suggests teaching children their civic duty as citizens? Why is this important?

~~~

~~~

question 10

The book briefly and effectively tackles the theme of common good. How does it make the theme of common good clear and understandable to readers? Is the way the parts and chapters arranged helpful?

~~~

~~~

question 11

He quotes political thinkers like Edmunde Burke, Vaclav Havel, and novelist George Orwell. What kind of ideas do these thinkers believe in?

~~~

~~~

question 12

Reich provides a long list of incidents that detail how public trust was repeatedly violated. What is the purpose of this list? What is your reaction as you read this list?

~~~

~~~

question 13

Reich provides interesting stories which serve to highlight his points, like when he discussed good leadership of Senator John McCain. What stories in the book do you particularly remember? Why?

~~~

question 14

He stresses that it is not color or language that makes the American identity. What does? Do you agree with him?

~~~

question 15

A list of recommended reading is provided at the end of the book, along with a discussion guide. What is the purpose of the reading list and discussion guide?

~~~

~~~

question 16

The New York Times Book Review thinks Reich's non-partisan view of the common good where readers are encouraged to think beyond party affiliations and political persuasion could be "too high-minded" and "so abstract." Do you agree? Why? Why not?

~~~

~~~

question 17

The Library Journal review says Reich's book is very timely. What is timely about it?

~~~

~~~

question 18

Kirkus review says the book is "provocative." What particularly about the book is provocative? Why?

~~~

~~~

question 19

Booklist says the book is a call for civic awareness that serves as a catalyst for conversations. How do you think readers would respond to the book's call for civic awareness? Why?

~~~

~~~

question 20

An Amazon review says the book is compelling and moved her to be angry. What emotion did you feel upon reading the book? Why?

~~~

Introducing the Author

Known for his expertise in public policy, University of California, Berkeley Professor Robert B. Reich has served three Presidents namely Gerald Ford, Jimmy Carter, and Bill Clinton under whom he was Labor Secretary from 1993 to 1997. He witnessed how the common good become increasingly irrelevant in the past 50 years, since he first started working at the office of Senator Robert F. Kennedy as a summer intern. He thinks reviving the common good might have to take another 50 years but believes it is worth doing it. Though he may probably not be there anymore to see it revitalized, he will continue to hope, because, quoting Reinhold Neibhur, he says hope must save us. Reich saw how common good was active during the early years. There was much generosity among people. Volunteering was very common. Donations were done often. People were always helping out during calamities. Today, he thinks civic life is nowhere near those times. It is because Americans don't feel connected to each other anymore, and the ideals have disappeared.

Reich has authored 15 books, among them best sellers like *Supercapitalism, Aftershock, Saving Capitalism*, and *The Work of Nations*. When not writing his books, he teaches public policy at UC Berkeley's Goldman School of Public Policy and at Blum Center for Developing Economies. He co-created the documentary *Saving Capitalism* and the film *Inequality for All. Time* cited him as one of the Ten Most Effective Cabinet Secretaries of the Twentieth Century. The *Wall Street Journal* named him one of the "Most Influential Business Thinkers in 2008. He is a much sought political commentator and has written for *The New Republic, The Atlantic, Harvard Business Review, The Wall Street Journal,* among others.

In *Saving Capitalism*, Reich tackles the question of how the American economic system is failing and how it could be saved. He explores the issues concerning the once wealthy middle class which is not prosperous anymore and the great disparity in wealth among classes that has become wider than ever. His book *Economics in Wonderland* is a collection of short essays on topics like student debt, gerrymandering, and social security, all accompanied by his doodles meant to illustrate his ideas. The book focuses on the topic of austerity and how the whole world is coping with it. *Aftershock* discusses the 2008 economic meltdown and the real reason behind it. Wall Street bankers were blamed for this catastrophe but Reich says the real problem is the disparity of wealth between the ultra-rich and the middle class. The economy is suffering because the middle class is prevented from having access to purchasing power to run a healthy economy. Reich suggests practical solutions that support a well-functioning society. *Beyond Outrage* discusses the ineffective political system that is paralyzing the American government, and how citizens can do something about it. The book provides a big picture of how wealth gap does not serve anybody else's interests except the few rich. He suggests mobilizing citizens to push for changes in government. A blueprint is provided to help citizens change the bleak future that awaits them.

Bonus Downloads
*Get Free Books with **Any Purchase** of* Conversation Starters!

Every purchase comes with a FREE download!

Add spice to any conversation
Never run out of things to say
Spend time with those you love

Get it Now

or Click Here.

Scan Your Phone

Fireside Questions

"What would you do?"

Tip: These questions can be a fun exercise as it spurs creativity among the readers by allowing alternate scene endings and "if this was you" questions.

~~~

question 21

Robert B. Reich has served three Presidents. How has common good changed over the years through different administrations?

~~~

~~~

question 22

He thinks reviving the common good might have to take another 50 years but believes it is worth doing it. Why?

~~~

~~~

question 23

Reich has authored 15 books, among them best sellers like *Supercapitalism, Aftershock, Saving Capitalism,* and *The Work of Nations*. What is a common theme in his books?

~~~

~~~

question 24

He is a much sought political commentator and has written for *The New Republic, The Atlantic, Harvard Business Review, The Wall Street Journal,* among others. Have you read his articles in these publications? What ideas of his do you particularly remember?

~~~

question 25

Beyond Outrage discusses the ineffective political system that is paralyzing the American government, and how citizens can do something about it. Is this theme somehow related to *The Common Good*? In what way?

~~~

question 26

Reich starts the first chapter with the story of Martin Shkreli. If he started off with an inspiring story instead of the disappointing case of Shkreli, how would it have changed the book? Would you continue reading?

~~~

~~~

question 27

He tackles the theme of common good in 209 pages divided into three parts and ten chapters. If he made the book longer, with more parts and chapters, what would be good topics to add? Do you think it would still be a readable book?

~~~

~~~

question 28

A list of recommended reading is provided at the end of the book. If the readings were omitted, would it greatly affect the book's content? Would it still be a good book without it?

~~~

~~~

question 29

Reich provides a long list of incidents that detail how public trust was repeatedly violated. If the list is instead turned into stories that show dramatic consequences, how would it change the book? Would you like it better?

~~~

question 30

He quotes political thinkers like Edmunde Burke, Vaclav Havel, and novelist George Orwell. If he did not mention political thinkers, how will it change the book? Will it still be credible and persuasive?

Quiz Questions

"Ready to Announce the Winners?"

Tip: Create a leaderboard and track scores to see who gets the most correct answers. Winners required. Prizes optional.

quiz question 1

Reich disputes _____'s philosophy of selfishness that is upheld by many of today's leaders and says that to the contrary the country has witnessed common good in action in the years after World War II.

~~~

quiz question 2

The book is composed of _____ parts and ten chapters.

~~~

~ ~ ~

quiz question 3

One way of restoring common good is teaching _____ their civic duty as citizens who will uphold shared values and ideals.

~ ~ ~

quiz question 4

True or False: Part Two is titled "What Happened to the Common Good?" and includes three chapters on how selfishness among business and government leaders have increasingly become the norm from the 60's to the present.

quiz question 5

True or False: In discussing what good leadership is all about he tells the case of Senator John McCain, who flew to Washington from Arizona despite ongoing treatment for brain cancer, to vote against the repeal the Affordable Care Act of July 2017.

quiz question 6

True or False: Reich stresses that it is not color or language that makes the American identity but the commitment to the shared values that promote equal access to justice and economic opportunity.

~~~

quiz question 7

True or False: A list of recommended films is provided at the end of the book, along with a discussion guide.

~~~

~~~

quiz question 8

Reich witnessed how the common good become increasingly irrelevant in the past 50 years, since he first started working at the office of Senator _____ as a summer intern.

~~~

~~~

quiz question 9

Though he may probably not be there anymore to see the common good revitalized in the next 50 years, he will continue to hope, because, quoting the thinker _____, he says hope must save us.

~~~

~~~

quiz question 10

True or False: Reich has authored 15 books, among them best sellers like *Supercapitalism, Aftershock, Saving Capitalism,* and *The Work of Nations.*

~~~

quiz question 11

True or False: *Time* cited him as one of the Ten Most Effective Cabinet Secretaries of the Twentieth Century.

quiz question 12

True or False: His book *Economics in Wonderland* is a collection of short essays on topics like student debt, gerrymandering, and social security, all accompanied by his doodles meant to illustrate his ideas.

Quiz Answers

1. Ayn Rand
2. three
3. children
4. True
5. True
6. True
7. False
8. Robert F. Kennedy
9. Reinhold Neibhur
10. True
11. True
12. True

Ways to Continue Your Reading

EVERY month, our team runs through a wide selection of books to pick the best titles for readers and reading groups, and promotes these titles to our thousands of readers – sometimes with free downloads, sale dates, and additional brochures.

Click here to sign up for these benefits.

If you have not yet read the original work or would like to read it again, you can purchase the original book here.

Bonus Downloads
*Get Free Books with **Any Purchase** of* Conversation Starters!

Every purchase comes with a FREE download!

Add spice to any conversation
Never run out of things to say
Spend time with those you love

Get it Now

or Click Here.

Scan Your Phone

On the Next Page…

If you found this book helpful to your discussions and rate it a 4 or 5, please write us a review on the next page.

Any length would be fine but we'd appreciate hearing you more! We'd be very encouraged.

Till next time,

BookHabits

"*Loving Books is Actually a Habit*"

Lightning Source UK Ltd.
Milton Keynes UK
UKHW012348270519
343433UK00001B/118/P